Childhoods
*of the*
Presidents

# Ulysses S. Grant

# Childhoods
## *of the*
# *P*residents

# Ulysses S. Grant

**Bethanne Kelly Patrick**

**Mason Crest Publishers**
**Philadelphia**

Produced by OTTN Publishing, Stockton, New Jersey

**Mason Crest Publishers**
370 Reed Road
Broomall, PA 19008
www.masoncrest.com

First printing

1 3 5 7 9 8 6 4 2


Library of Congress Cataloging-in-Publication Data

Patrick, Bethanne Kelly.
    Ulysses S. Grant / Bethanne Patrick.
        p.   cm.   (Childhood of the presidents)
    Summary: A biography of the eighteenth president of the United
    States, focusing on his childhood and young adulthood.
    Includes bibliographical references (p. ) and index.
        ISBN 1-59084-276-6
    1. Grant, Ulysses S. (Ulysses Simpson), 1822-1885—Childhood
    and youth—Juvenile literature. 2. Grant, Ulysses S. (Ulysses
    Simpson), 1822-1885—Juvenile literature. 3. Presidents—United
    States—Biography—Juvenile literature. [1. Grant, Ulysses S.
    (Ulysses Simpson), 1822-1885—Childhood and youth.
    2. Presidents.] I. Title.  II. Series.
    E672.P27 2003
    973.8'2'092—dc21
    [B]                                                      2002069201

*Childhoods*
*of the*
*Presidents*

# *Table of Contents*

★★★★★★★★★★★★★★★★★

# ★ *Introduction* ★

Alexis de Tocqueville began his great work *Democracy in America* with a discourse on childhood. If we are to understand the prejudices, the habits and the passions that will rule a man's life, Tocqueville said, we must watch the baby in his mother's arms; we must see the first images that the world casts upon the mirror of his mind; we must hear the first words that awaken his sleeping powers of thought. "The entire man," he wrote, "is, so to speak, to be seen in the cradle of the child."

That is why these books on the childhoods of the American presidents are so much to the point. And, as our history shows, a great variety of childhoods can lead to the White House. The record confirms the ancient adage that every American boy, no matter how unpromising his beginnings, can aspire to the presidency. Soon, one hopes, the adage will be extended to include every American girl.

All our presidents thus far have been white males who, within the limits of their gender, reflect the diversity of American life. They were born in nineteen of our states; eight of the last thirteen presidents were born west of the Mississippi. Of all our presidents, Abraham Lincoln had the least promising childhood, yet he became our greatest president. Oddly enough, presidents who are children of privilege sometimes feel an obligation to reform society in order to give children of poverty a better break. And, with Lincoln the great exception, presidents who are children of poverty sometimes feel that there is no need to reform a society that has enabled them to rise from privation to the summit.

Does schooling make a difference? Harry S. Truman, the only twentieth-century president never to attend college, is generally accounted a near-great president. Actually nine—more than one fifth—of our presidents never went to college at all, including such luminaries as George Washington, Andrew Jackson and Grover Cleveland. But, Truman aside, all the non-college men held the highest office before the twentieth century, and, given the increasing complexity of life, a college education will unquestionably be a necessity in the twenty-first century.

Every reader of this book, girls included, has a right to aspire to the presidency. As you survey the childhoods of those who made it, try to figure out the qualities that brought them to the White House. I would suggest that among those qualities are ambition, determination, discipline, education—and luck.

*—ARTHUR M. SCHLESINGER, JR.*

General Ulysses S. Grant at the Battle of the Wilderness, May 1864. As head of all the Union armies, Grant practiced a grim, relentless approach to defeating the South that won him the nickname "Unconditional Surrender."

# *Strengths and Shortcomings*

When he was about eight years old, Ulysses Grant—who loved horses—desperately wanted a colt owned by a man named Robert Ralston. Ralston, who lived a few miles outside Ulysses's hometown of Georgetown, Ohio, had offered to sell the horse to the boy's father. But Jesse Grant thought the asking price of $25 was too high. Still, Ulysses was single-minded in his determination to have the colt. He begged and pestered his father relentlessly.

Years later, looking back on his famous life, Ulysses S. Grant would write about that boyhood experience in his *memoirs*. "My father yielded," he recalled, "but said twenty dollars was all the horse was worth, and told me to offer that price; if it was not accepted I was to offer twenty-two and a half, and if that would not get him, to give the twenty-five. I at once mounted a horse and went for the colt. When I got to Mr. Ralston's house, I said to him: 'Papa says I may offer you twenty dollars for the colt, but if you won't take that, I am to offer twenty-two and a half, and if you won't take that, I am to give you twenty-five.'" Needless to say, Ralston agreed to part with the animal only for the full $25.

The way eight-year-old Ulysses Grant came to own Robert Ralston's colt certainly makes for a humorous tale. But the story also provides a glimpse at the character of an important figure in American history—a major Civil War general and, later, America's 18th president. Perhaps, too, the qualities that would lead to a string of business and political failures for the adult Ulysses Grant can be detected in the actions of the boy.

Just as the child's doggedness eventually wore down his father, enabling him to get the colt he wanted, the adult Ulysses Grant's doggedness eventually wore down the South, bringing the Civil War to an end. As a strategist, Grant was capable if not brilliant. His strength as a general lay in his single-minded determination. Nothing—not even huge numbers of *casualties*—deterred him from his objective.

No one expects eight-year-olds to have the sophistication necessary to understand the motivations of adults, so it's no surprise that the young Ulysses failed in his attempt to bargain with Ralston. Interestingly, though, the adult Ulysses Grant was—like the child trying to buy a colt that had caught his eye—direct, honest, and unskilled at manipulating others. Throughout his life he also seems to have had difficulty in judging people—or at least in deciding which people could be trusted. His presidency was tainted by a host of scandals involving his close advisers, even though Grant himself remained honest. And toward the end of his life, when he should have been financially secure, he lost all his money after the failure of a firm in which he'd invested heavily—and whose officers happened to be crooked.

Of course, it's impossible to understand Ulysses S. Grant

without knowing about his parents. His father, Jesse R. Grant of Deerfield, Ohio, was one of eight children born to Captain Noah Grant and his second wife, Rachel, in the space of just 11 years. When his wife died, Noah Grant—poor and with so many mouths to feed—was forced to *apprentice* his older boys. Jesse was only 11 when he was sent to work on a farm about 25 miles away. Two years later, he began to learn the leather-making trade as an apprentice in Maysville, Kentucky. He soon returned to Ohio, though, because Kentucky was slave-owning territory. He said, "I would not own slaves and I would not live where there were slaves and not own them."

In 1821, at the age of 27 and now the owner of a *tannery*, Jesse Grant married 23-year-old Hannah Simpson of Point Pleasant, Ohio. Hannah, who was quiet and reserved, came from an upstanding family that had farmed in the area for several generations. She was also a devout Methodist, with views against slavery like Jesse's.

The couple moved into a two-room house with a fireplace at one end overlooking the Ohio River. On April 27, 1822, their first child was born. The baby was a strapping boy who weighed more than 10 pounds. The Grants didn't name him immediately, but discussed many options before choosing "Hiram" (which Hannah's father liked) and "Ulysses," after Jesse's favorite literary character. Throughout his childhood the Grants called him Ulysses or Lyss.

> The name Ulysses comes from the Roman translation of a Greek epic poem, Homer's *Odyssey*. In that poem the hero, Odysseus, or Ulysses, struggles to make his way home to Greece after fighting in the Trojan War.

From his early childhood Ulysses Grant demonstrated an extraordinary gift for understanding and working with horses. He could readily tame even the wildest.

# A Way with Horses

In 1824 Jesse Grant moved his family to Georgetown, Ohio, where he built a small brick house and a tannery. When Ulysses was still a toddler, a traveling circus came to town. The circus concluded with a pony show, at the end of which the ringmaster asked, "Who will ride the pony?" Little Ulysses begged so hard to be allowed on the animal that his parents relented, and he "held on the steed's back, and rode two or three times round the ring, manifesting more glee than he had ever shown before."

Very early on, Ulysses demonstrated that he had an extraordinary way with horses. At his father's tannery, according to family stories, he crawled around the feet of the large horses, swung on their tails, and played beneath them in their stalls. This behavior would normally be quite dangerous: when startled, horses will rear and kick, and they can easily kill a person, especially a small child. But the Grants apparently didn't worry about Ulysses because, as his mother remarked, "Horses seem to understand Ulysses." And Ulysses clearly understood horses.

His father allowed him from a very early age to ride full-grown horses and even to stand on their backs as they trotted along. In an interview later in his life, Jesse Grant remembered, "At eight or nine he would ride them at the top of their speed, he standing upon one foot and balancing himself by the bridle reins." Although Ulysses played at things that amused the children of his day, such as sledding, skating, fishing, and swimming, he was truly fascinated by horses and appeared happiest when riding or working with the animals. "Perhaps it was my son's taste for horses and the great pleasure he took in riding and driving," Jesse Grant said, "that prevented his ever becoming addicted, so much as most boys, to other amusements. I do not know that he ever cared for any others at all, except playing marbles; of that he was extremely fond."

Ulysses, short and chubby as a boy, could tame almost any horse, no matter how large or wild it was. Apparently he was able to size up a horse's temperament the way some people can quickly read the personalities of strangers from subtle clues. This unusual ability was on display whenever a circus came to town. For a five-dollar reward, circuses of the time would invite spectators to try to ride ponies specially trained to stop, start, and buck in attempts to unseat anyone who mounted them. When the ringmaster asked, "Who will ride this pony?" Georgetown residents knew

**Ulysses Grant's almost-magical gift for taming horses was a valuable skill. On 19th-century farms, horses were important for work and transportation. Those who could handle them easily were much admired.**

what to expect: Ulysses Grant would come forward, having silently studied the pony's movements during the show. The

The birthplace of Hiram Ulysses Grant. The two-room frame house in Point Pleasant, Ohio, overlooked a river.

boy would confidently mount the animal and hang on, "not a muscle" of his face moving. Before long, the ringmaster or the clown would end up handing over the promised prize.

Although he was a quiet child who spent a good deal of time alone, Ulysses always seemed to have faith in his abilities. His father recalled: "He never seemed inclined to put himself forward at all; and was modest, retiring and *reticent*,

As a boy, Ulysses performed a variety of tasks on his family's small farm, including, as he later recalled, "all the work done with horses, such as breaking up the land, furrowing, ploughing corn and potatoes, bringing in the crops when harvested, [and] hauling all the wood."

as he is now. But he never appeared to have distrust in himself, or any misgivings about his ability to do anything which could be expected of a boy of his size and age."

Although children in the 19th century were generally given more responsibility at a younger age than are today's children, Ulysses was unusually self-reliant even for his day. To make extra money, Jesse Grant allowed his oldest son—beginning when the boy was only 10—to use a team of horses and a wagon to carry passengers as far away as Cincinnati, a full 35 miles from Georgetown. Ulysses liked the job because it combined horses and travel, both of which he loved. He seemed to have no fear about traveling back through dense woods or on dark roads by himself. But he did develop one superstitious habit that would remain with him all his life: no matter how far out of his way it forced him to go, Ulysses would not back-track or retrace his steps. If he went too far, he found an alter-nate route, usually somewhat roundabout, to take him to his destination.

Once, when Ulysses was about 12 years old, he drove a pair of horses a distance of 12 miles and was asked to stay overnight so that he could bring two women back to Georgetown. The return route crossed a creek that had risen during the night to the height of the horses' middles. In mid-stream, the horses began to get agitated and the frightened passengers started screaming. As his father later related the incident, Ulysses looked back from the driver's seat and said calmly, "Don't speak. I will take you through safe," which he did. This self-possession and quiet confidence would later be seen in the general on the battlefield, who didn't so much as flinch even as shells exploded around him.

Though horses were his passion and he might have pre-ferred to spend all his time riding and working with them, Ulysses Grant's parents made him and their other children (Jesse and Hannah Grant eventually had two more boys and three girls) attend school. Jesse Grant himself had an intense thirst for knowledge. Family cir-cumstances had prevented him from getting more than

Evening entertainment in the Midwest during the 19th century was quiet, mostly reading and conver-sation. However, there was usually work that could still be done. Boys of Ulysses Grant's day would roll strips of newspaper into "spills," long cones that could be used to light fires in an era when matches and candles were expensive.

six months of formal schooling, but as his son Ulysses would write, he "was a constant reader up to the day of his death—in his eightieth year." And the scarcity of available books gave him the "habit of studying everything he read, so that when he got through with a book, he knew everything in it." Jesse Grant was determined that his children—particularly his oldest son—would receive the education that he was never able to get.

At the time, the typical education involved instruction in reading, writing, and arithmetic in a one-room schoolhouse with classmates of varying ages. Local schoolmasters were often not particularly qualified.

Ulysses Grant was an unremarkable student. Math was his best subject; he struggled with spelling and the rules of grammar.

He apparently didn't like school very much either—and the reason seems not to have been simply that he would rather spend his time riding and driving horses. Schoolteachers of the day frequently resorted to *corporal punishment* to discipline their pupils. When Ulysses encountered the schoolteacher's "long beech switch" he was horrified. "The rod was freely used there," Grant later remembered, "and I was not *exempt* from its influence."

**Early American Methodists were strongly anti-slavery, and the Methodist Church was one of the first to have African-American clergy. From 1821 on, the church forbade its members to own slaves.**

At least part of his shock at being beaten by teachers can be explained by his experience at home. Although Jesse and Hannah Grant do

An engraving of Hannah Simpson Grant, from a photo taken late in her life. The mother of the Union's top general was an ardent Methodist and a staunch abolitionist.

not seem to have shown their children much outward affection, they rarely scolded, and there is no indication that they ever hit their kids—unlike many other parents of the time. As long as Ulysses completed his chores obediently, his parents allowed him freedom to play. The Grants' low-key parenting may have had something to do with their religious devotion: Jesse Grant had become as ardent a Methodist as his wife, a leader in church affairs and a host to every preacher who rode the circuit from town to town in the Ohio countryside.

TANNING.

Workers in a tannery prepare animal hides for the leather industry. "I detested the trade," Ulysses Grant would write of his father's tanning business, "preferring almost any other labor."

# The Reluctant Tanner

S chool, Ulysses wrote, "did not exempt me from labor." In this his childhood was typical for the time. Besides his tannery, Jesse Grant did some farming. He also owned 50 acres of forest where "choppers were employed to cut enough wood to last a twelve-month." As soon as Ulysses was old enough to help haul the wood, he did. When he was a little older, he helped to load it. Later still, he recalled, "I was strong enough to hold a plough," and "until seventeen I did all the work done with horses, such as breaking up the land, furrowing, ploughing corn and potatoes, bringing in the crops when harvested, hauling all the wood, besides tending two or three horses, a cow or two, and sawing wood for stoves, etc., while still attending school."

Most youths of the day learned how to work from their fathers, older brothers, and other relatives and neighbors, combining the chores of farm life with a few weeks of school in the winter until they reached their teenage years. At 14, most boys stopped their schooling, leaving with basic skills of reading and writing and some simple arithmetic.

Youths then moved on to apprenticeship, clerking in a

store, or "working out" as a farm laborer—or they stayed home to work on the farm. At 16 or 17, depending upon their health and ambition, young men were performing many of the tasks of adult males.

Before they married, most young men—and many young women—had lived away from home. But when they went to other communities to work as farm laborers or household helpers, serve as apprentices, work in a mill or shop, or teach school, they were not completely independent. They lived in the households of their employers or boarded with others in the community. Not until they were married and living in their own households were young people considered fully independent.

Young people left school, left home, or began working for others at widely different ages, depending upon their skills and inclinations, their family situations, and their parents' wealth. Some boys (particularly those who disliked farming) were apprenticed to skilled craftsmen, but some sons could not be spared by their parents and had to work at home until they were of adult age and their fathers could make no legal claim on them.

At the age when their brothers were beginning to help their fathers in the fields or barns, girls who lived on farms began to share the responsibilities of their mothers and older female relatives. These responsibilities included caring for younger children, preparing food, producing clothing, and helping to make butter and cheese. Girls were sometimes able to attend school for a season or two longer than boys, because there were fewer ways in which their labor could be made directly profitable to their families.

An undated photograph of Ulysses Grant's father, Jesse. Though he was by trade a tanner, Jesse Grant never tried to force his oldest son to follow in his footsteps.

If they had missed the usual early apprenticeship age, some young men took on informal apprentice or training arrangements with tradesmen or craftsmen. Others stayed with their families, inheriting or receiving land or a business to make a gradual transition to independence and farm or business ownership.

For the Grant family, a natural progression would have been for Ulysses to be trained in and to take over his father's tannery. Very early on, however, the firstborn Grant began to show his distaste for his father's business. "I detested the trade," he wrote, "preferring almost any other labor."

Work in the tannery was hot, noisy, and, above all, smelly. The process of making animal hides into leather required many steps: scraping, soaking, liming, and more soaking with harsh substances, to name a few. The tanning process was extremely important in leather making, because tannin (the critical substance in the process) changes leather from an

At Richardson and Rand's academy in Georgetown, Ohio, Ulysses Grant overcame his fear of public speaking and made considerable progress in other academic areas. Unfortunately, financial considerations forced him to leave the school after a year.

organic material into one that will not carry bacteria. Since leather was needed for everything from saddles to boots to luggage, tanneries were kept very busy.

Part of Ulysses's job early on was to keep the hopper that ground bark for the tannery filled with wood. (Bark contains large amounts of tannin.) He would hire any friend he could find, boy or girl, to take over this job for him—but he was not above paying them only a fraction of what he earned from his father!

Ulysses hated the smells and sights of the tannery. His love of horses probably didn't help. As one biographer has noted, "Jesse [Grant] regarded horses as a source of hides for his business," whereas Ulysses "saw them as wonderfully differentiated individuals." It seemed to genuinely pain the boy to see old horses, and cows and steers, killed so their hides could be turned into leather. For all of his life, in fact, he was a reluctant meat-eater, only dining on cuts that had been cooked to an almost unrecognizable state. He also hated to hunt.

If Ulysses didn't relish the thought of spending his life as a tanner, his father wasn't going to try to force him. In fact, at a time when few parents saw that their sons were educated after about age 14—and those who did were almost always wealthy and had an eye on college for their boys—Jesse Grant sent his eldest son to a private academy in Maysville, Kentucky. Ulysses, 14 at the time, stayed with an aunt in Maysville while attending Richardson and Rand's academy for the 1836–37 school year.

> Many plants and barks contain a bitter ingredient called tannin, which combines with proteins to form a compound that will not rot or decompose easily. The principal sources of tannin are leaves, nuts, and bark and wood from oak, hemlock, chestnut, and various other types of trees.

Although the boy had not been particularly studious at home in Georgetown, he made some progress at Richardson and Rand's. He overcame his fear of public speaking and learned some principles of debate.

Unfortunately, Jesse Grant, though he managed to get by financially, was never rich. After one school year, Ulysses had to return to Georgetown. But soon an opportunity for further education of the eldest Grant son—at no cost to the family—would present itself.

# A Quiet Cadet

*T*he United States Military Academy at West Point, New York, was established by America's third president, Thomas Jefferson, in 1802. The mission of the academy, which is often referred to simply as West Point, was—and is—to educate future army officers for the nation. To gain entry into West Point, a young man must be nominated by a congressman or senator from his state. Only two nominees are accepted per state each year, so admission is extremely competitive. If accepted, the youth attends West Point tuition-free. In fact, the government pays all the *cadet's* living expenses.

The Grants had heard a great deal about West Point because one of Ulysses's closest friends, Daniel Ammen, was going there. In fact, Daniel's brother Jacob Ammen was a member of the academy's faculty.

When Bartlett Bailey, the son of Georgetown's richest fam-

Located along the Hudson River about 50 miles north of New York City, the United States Military Academy at West Point has, since the early 1800s, prepared young men to become officers in the U.S. Army. Sixteen-year-old Ulysses Grant entered West Point in 1839, about 22 years before this illustration was made.

ily, was dismissed from West Point, Jesse Grant saw an opportunity for his oldest boy to obtain a coveted appointment to West Point. Without telling Ulysses, he arranged for an Ohio congressman named Thomas Hamer to nominate his son.

As he looked back on events, Ulysses would write that he wasn't sure his father knew whether he'd accept an appointment to West Point. That may be why Jesse Grant suddenly decided to suggest a much less pleasant option first. In 1838, Jesse said he had a shortage of workers and told Ulysses he needed him to help in the tannery.

Ulysses reluctantly agreed, but said, "Father, this tanning is not the kind of work I like. I'll work at it though, if you wish me to, until I am twenty-and-one; but you can depend on it, I'll never work a day at it after that."

Jesse replied that he wanted his son to "work at whatever you like and intend to follow. Now, what do you think you would like?" After discussing a few options, Jesse asked, "How would you like West Point?" According to his recollection, Ulysses replied, "First rate."

And so, in late 1838, 16-year-old Hiram Ulysses Grant left Georgetown, Ohio, bound for the Hudson Valley in New York. The journey was exciting. He traveled in a canal boat over the Allegheny Mountains and took his first train ride, from Harrisburg, Pennsylvania, to Philadelphia. He had relatives in Philadelphia and stayed with them for about a week, exploring the historic city and attending the theater. Then he proceeded north to New York City, which he explored on his own for several days. Finally, he made the last leg of his journey, by steamboat and train up the Hudson River valley to West Point.

Artillery practice at the United States Military Academy. Initially, Ulysses Grant disliked his experience at West Point. "A military life," he recalled, "had no charms for me, and I had not the faintest idea of staying in the army even if I should be graduated, which I did not expect."

When he arrived at the United States Military Academy he signed himself Ulysses H. Grant, inverting his first and middle names. He'd always been called Ulysses, and now he did not wish his initials to spell "H. U. G." He discovered, though, that Congressman Hamer had erroneously nominated him under the name Ulysses Simpson Grant, Simpson being his mother's maiden name. Ulysses didn't bother to correct the mistake. When his fellow cadets saw the initials "U. S. Grant," they jokingly began to call him "Uncle Sam." The "Sam" stuck—in his early army years, Ulysses would be known as Captain Sam Grant.

At 5 foot 1 inch tall, Ulysses was just an inch over the United States Military Academy minimum for entry. Now 117 pounds, he was no longer a chubby boy, but physically he wasn't very impressive.

Ulysses had come to West Point doubtful about his future as an army leader. "A military life," he wrote in his memoirs,

A portrait of Thomas "Stonewall" Jackson, who was a few years behind Ulysses Grant at West Point. Jackson and Grant would fight on different sides during the Civil War. Other cadets who studied with Grant and later became generals for the South included Simon Bolivar Buckner and James Longstreet. Buckner surrendered a force of 14,000 men to Grant in 1862; Longstreet was present at Appomattox Court House when Grant took Robert E. Lee's surrender to end the war.

"had no charms for me, and I had not the faintest idea of staying in the army even if I should be graduated, which I did not expect." In fact, in 1839, when Congress considered a bill to abolish the military academy, Ulysses "read the debates with much interest," secretly hoping the bill would pass. He found classes "wearisome and uninteresting," but he managed to do fairly well. He excelled in mathematics but had some trouble with French. By his second year, he ranked 10th in a class of 53. "I never succeeded in getting squarely at either end of my class, in any one study during the four years," Ulysses recalled.

Still, he eventually began to like West Point a bit more. He was always quiet and reserved, though. In fact, years later, when Ulysses had become the most celebrated general in the United States, many of the men who had gone through the academy with him were unable to recall anything significant about what the cadet from Ohio had done at West Point. By the end of his final year, Ulysses's class rank stood right in the middle: 21 out of 39. His academic performance had been completely unremarkable.

Nor had he excelled at athletics. Although he'd grown half a foot during his four years at West Point, standing 5 feet 7 inches at graduation, Ulysses had been too slightly built for most sports. The one area he did stand out in, not surprisingly, was horse riding.

During the June 1843 graduation exercises, West Pointers performed maneuvers on horseback for their audience of family members, friends, and distinguished guests. When the initial display was finished, a silence descended and everyone waited for what would come next.

Sergeant Herschberger, the riding master, put the jump bar on its highest rung and barked out, "Cadet Grant!" A slender cadet on an enormous horse dashed out and began to gallop toward the bar. A murmur arose among the cadets and West Point community, who began telling their guests that the small figure was on York, a powerful animal known for his *obstinacy* and strength. Only U. S. Grant and one other classmate could even mount the horse. After a long and thunderous gallop, the horse and its rider rose as if one and flew over the bar. A cadet spectator said it was "as if man and beast had been welded together."

Herschberger yelled out, "Very well done, sir! Class dismissed." Ulysses Grant's high-jump record with York (no one knows if it was set that day, or earlier) stood at West Point for 25 years.

The Union's most prominent military hero, Ulysses Grant rode his enormous popularity to the White House, winning election as the 18th president in 1868.

# War and Politics

*A*lthough he had graduated from the United States Military Academy, Ulysses S. Grant had no intention of pursuing a military career. He planned to resign from the army after he had completed his required tour of duty as a second lieutenant. No doubt he was bitterly disappointed at his assignment. A natural horseman, he had hoped to be assigned to a *cavalry* unit. Instead, the army had placed him with the *infantry*. Ulysses, now 23 years old, moved to Jefferson *Barracks* near St. Louis, Missouri, to serve in the Fourth U.S. Infantry.

The United States Army of the 1840s was a small one, with about 7,000 men. Ulysses was assigned as quartermaster, or supply officer, to a *regiment* just south of St. Louis. His West Point roommate, Frederick Dent, was posted there too. Dent had grown up nearby, and he took Ulysses home with him one day and introduced him to his sister, Julia Dent. Julia was warm and sociable, and Ulysses fell for her immediately. She didn't feel the same way about him at first. In fact, when he was reassigned to another post, many of his early letters to her went unanswered. Over time, however, she took to him, and their mutual devotion was total. Julia would stick by Ulysses through many difficult times, seeing qualities in him that no one else recognized.

In September 1845, Lieutenant Grant and the Fourth Infantry were sent to Corpus Christi, Texas, as war was brewing with Mexico over Mexican territory the United States wanted to acquire. Fighting broke out the following year and ended in 1848 with Mexico's defeat. Although he was a supply officer, Ulysses became involved in several battles, and he was twice cited for bravery. But he would always believe that the United States had provoked the unjustified war, and in his memoirs he even speculated that the Civil War was God's punishment upon America for starting the Mexican War. War's cheerless terrors also led him to begin smoking and drinking, occasionally to excess, and these habits would stay with him throughout his life.

In 1848, promoted to captain, he was sent back to the Missouri posting, and he married Julia Dent. Because Julia's family owned slaves, Jesse and Hannah Grant refused to attend their son's wedding. Their snub of the Dent family would pain Ulysses for the rest of his life. He and Julia eventually raised three sons and a daughter.

Meanwhile, army life wasn't working out for Ulysses. Being transferred from one lonely base to the next for six years, away from his family, worsened an early drinking problem. He quarreled with his army superiors and eventually resigned.

Returning to Missouri with his wife and children, Ulysses tried to farm some land Julia's father gave them, building a

A view of the Battle of Buena Vista, February 23, 1847. Though he was a supply officer during the Mexican War, Ulysses Grant twice won citations for bravery. Still, he viewed the entire conflict as a shameful attempt by the United States to seize Mexican land.

sturdy but unattractive home he called Hardscrabble. He tried a half-dozen other lines of work over the next half-dozen years and utterly failed at every one. By 1860, at the age of 38, he was forced to work for his younger brother in a leather shop in Galena, Illinois.

In 1861, however, the Civil War broke out as 11 states in the South *seceded* from the Union and formed the *Confederacy*. The issue that now divided the nation was the same one that had led to the split between Ulysses and his parents when he married Julia Dent: slavery. The Confederate states weren't about to permit the newly elected president, Abraham Lincoln, to impose his *abolitionist* beliefs upon them.

Many of the southern-born officers with whom Ulysses Grant had attended West Point resigned from the army and took up commissions in the service of the Confederacy. In the Union, experienced fighting men were now in short supply, and the army took Ulysses back as a colonel—but not for a choice assignment. Instead of commanding a regular army unit, Ulysses was ordered to train volunteers. He drilled the First Illinois Volunteers nearly to death and led them in several successful raids against Confederate guerrilla bands. He had a new lease on life—and was promoted to brigadier general of volunteers.

Ulysses Grant's calm during battle astounded everyone who witnessed it—although it probably wouldn't have surprised his Georgetown family and friends who had seen the young Ulysses tame the wildest of horses. The closest bursting enemy shell couldn't make him flinch; he just quietly issued orders while puffing cigar after cigar.

In the early years of the Civil War, the generals of the Confederacy consistently outperformed their Union counterparts. Frustrated, President Abraham Lincoln replaced a succession of commanders with whom he was dissatisfied. In particular, Lincoln couldn't tolerate what he considered the overly cautious approach of some of his generals. To the president, these men seemed more interested in avoiding casualties rather than in carrying the fight to the Confederates. In the western theater of the war, though, Ulysses Grant scored several victories that would bring him to the attention of the president and lead to promotions.

Lincoln was approached with complaints about the appalling number of casualties among Grant's men and Grant's drinking problem. But he responded sharply, saying, "I cannot spare this man—he fights!"

By 1864, Lincoln had put Ulysses Grant in charge of all the Union armies. Coordinating the movements of the generals under his command, Ulysses applied relentless pressure to the

This photograph shows Ulysses Grant at his field headquarters during the Civil War. As a commander, Grant was personally fearless and had a gift for being able to grasp quickly what was happening on a battlefield.

Confederates. Losses were high on both sides, but eventually the South was worn down. Ulysses trapped the main Confederate army south of Richmond, Virginia, and forced its surrender in April of 1865 at Appomattox Court House, ending the conflict.

In four years he had gone from a failure to the most revered soldier in the Union. In 1866 he was named general of the armies, a rank that had been achieved by no one other than George Washington.

Lincoln's assassination at the end of the Civil War thrust the ineffective Andrew Johnson into the presidency. Johnson's moderate approach didn't suit the Radical Republicans, who wanted to protect the rights of newly freed blacks in the South and who demanded that the rebellious Southern states meet strict conditions before they would be readmitted into the Union. The Radical Republicans backed Grant as a presidential candidate in 1868.

In his acceptance of the nomination the general famously said, "Let us have peace." With his enormous popularity throughout the country, he easily defeated Democrat Horatio Seymour in the election to become America's 18th president. In 1872 he would win reelection to a second term.

In his inaugural address, Ulysses Grant said he wanted to ensure voting rights regardless of "race, color or previous condition of servitude." He appears to have been genuinely concerned about the condition of African Americans (and about the fate of all the nation's poor). But his plans for guaranteeing fair treatment for blacks failed. In the South particularly, African Americans—though freed from the bonds of slavery—continued to suffer unequal treatment and intimidation by whites.

Ulysses Grant's good intentions were undermined by his political inexperience, which began to show almost

> **Ulysses Grant was one of a handful of presidents with the rank of general. Others included George Washington, Zachary Taylor, Andrew Jackson, and Dwight D. Eisenhower.**

immediately after he assumed office. Haunted by his early failures, he was too loyal to anyone who had shown him kindness. He appointed friends to various posts, and many of them were incompetent or corrupt. His administration was plagued by a series of scandals. Historians generally agree that Ulysses S. Grant was not a very successful president.

After leaving office in 1877, Ulysses and Julia embarked on a world tour, receiving warm welcomes wherever they went. When they returned to the United States two years later, the response of their countrymen was equally enthusiastic. Despite the failures of his presidency, Ulysses S. Grant remained a hero to his fellow Americans.

Unfortunately, he wasn't able to enjoy his fame in comfort. He invested his money—along with his good name—in a Wall Street firm, Grant & Ward. In May 1884, after some questionable dealings by its partners, the company collapsed, leaving Ulysses Grant not only penniless but also deep in debt. Creditors swarmed; a close friend even sued him. Worst of all, Ulysses was not well. Decades of smoking had caught up with him: he had cancer of the throat and was dying.

As determined as ever, he set out to right his financial situation so that he could provide for his family. His novelist

Ulysses Grant with his wife, the former Julia Dent, and their son Jesse. The photograph was taken in 1872, the year Grant won reelection to the presidency.

friend Mark Twain urged Ulysses to write his memoirs. Ulysses approached this task with the same calm self-possession he had demonstrated on the battlefields of the Civil War. Perhaps because he knew he was dying, he didn't try to gloss over his shortcomings. He freely admitted to his many mistakes as well as noting his triumphs.

In its later stages the cancer robbed Ulysses of his voice, making it impossible to dictate the memoirs to an assistant.

His last days were spent on his porch with pencil and paper, wrapped in blankets and in fearsome pain, slowly scrawling out his life's epic tale.

On July 23, 1885, just days after he'd completed the book, Ulysses Simpson Grant died at his home in Mount McGregor, New York. *The Personal Memoirs of U. S. Grant*, published by Mark Twain, turned out to be a huge success and provided for the financial security of the Grant family.

The funeral of Ulysses S. Grant, held in New York City and attended by thousands, was as epic as his memoirs. America honored the man who had fought for and helped save the Union by constructing a large tomb and memorial on Riverside Drive. Buried there alongside his beloved Julia, who died in 1902, rests the body of the horseman, soldier, and statesman Ulysses Simpson Grant.

# CHRONOLOGY

**1822**   Hiram Ulysses Grant is born on April 27 at Point Pleasant, Clermont County, Ohio.

**1823**   Moves with his family to Georgetown, Brown County, Ohio.

**1836**   Attends academy of Richardson and Rand in Maysville, Kentucky.

**1838**   Receives appointment to the United States Military Academy at West Point; when he arrives there the following year, discovers he has been registered as "Ulysses S. Grant."

**1843**   Graduates from West Point 21st out of 39 cadets and receives rank of second lieutenant.

**1846**   Assigned to General Zachary Taylor's regiment during the Mexican War.

**1848**   Marries Julia Boggs Dent.

**1854**   Resigns from the army with the rank of captain.

**1855 –61**   Moves his family back to the Midwest and endures several years of setbacks as he tries to make a living as a farmer at Hardscrabble, a home he builds.

**1861**   At the outbreak of the Civil War, receives a rank of colonel of volunteers for the Seventh District Regiment, Illinois.

**1862**   Appointed major general of volunteers by President Lincoln.

**1863**   After his victory at Vicksburg, appointed major general in the regular army.

**1864**   Promoted to lieutenant general, a rank reinstated just for him, and given command of all Union armies.

**1865**   Accepts surrender of General Robert E. Lee at Appomattox Court House, Virginia, on April 9; awarded rank of general of the armies.

**1869**   Inaugurated as 18th president of the United States.

**1872**   Reelected.

**1885**   While ill with throat cancer, writes autobiography, *Personal Memoirs of U. S. Grant*; dies at his home in Mount McGregor, New York, on July 23.

# GLOSSARY

**abolitionist**—characterized by anti-slavery beliefs; or a person who advocates the outlawing of slavery.

**apprentice**—to set a person (usually a boy) to work under an agreement with a tradesman or craftsman; or a person learning a trade, art, or craft through practical experience under skilled people.

**barracks**—buildings made to house soldiers on one site, such as an army post.

**cadet**—a student at a service academy, usually being trained for an officer's commission.

**casualties**—soldiers who are killed or wounded during combat.

**cavalry**—an army unit that fights on horseback.

**Confederacy**—the 11 states that seceded, or withdrew, from the Union in 1861, touching off the Civil War.

**corporal punishment**—physical punishment, such as spanking or striking with a belt or switch.

**exempt**—not subject to; free from a restriction, duty, or punishment.

**infantry**—an army unit that fights on foot.

**memoirs**—a narrative of personal experience.

**obstinacy**—stubbornness.

**regiment**—a large military unit.

**reticent**—reserved or quiet; reluctant.

**secede**—to withdraw from an organization, alliance, or nation.

**tannery**—a place where animal hides are converted into leather through the use of tannin.

# FURTHER READING

Bently, Bill. *Ulysses S. Grant*. Philadelphia: Franklin Watts, 1993.

Fuller, J. F. C. *General Grant, A Biography for Young Americans*. New York: Da Capo Press, 1932.

Lewis, Lloyd. *Captain Sam Grant*. Boston: Little, Brown and Company, 1950.

Marrin, Albert. *Unconditional Surrender: U. S. Grant and the Civil War*. New York: Atheneum Press, 1994.

Patrick, Bethanne. *Abraham Lincoln*. Philadelphia: Mason Crest Publishers, 2003.

Welsbacher, Anne. *Ulysses S. Grant*. Edina, Minn.: Abdo & Daughters, 2001.

- http://www.mscomm.com/~ulysses
  A comprehensive U. S. Grant website.

- http://home.nycap.rr.com/history/grant.html
  Grant's *Memoirs* on-line.

- http://www.ipl.org/ref/POTUS/USGrant.html
  A brief biography of Grant, plus links.

- http://www.historychannel.com/tdih/civilwar.html
  A day-by-day guide to the Civil War.

- http://www.nps.gov/gegrt
  Grant's Tomb.

# INDEX

# PICTURE CREDITS

# *Contributors*

ARTHUR M. SCHLESINGER JR. holds the Albert
Schweitzer Chair in the Humanities at the
Graduate Center of the City University of
New York. He is the author of more than a
dozen books, including *The Age of Jackson*;
*The Vital Center*; *The Age of Roosevelt* (3 vols.);
*A Thousand Days: John F. Kennedy in the White
House*; *Robert Kennedy and His Times*; *The
Cycles of American History*; and *The Imperial
Presidency*. Professor Schlesinger served as
Special Assistant to President Kennedy (1961–63). His numerous
awards include the Pulitzer Prize for History; the Pulitzer Prize for
Biography; two National Book Awards; the Bancroft Prize; and the
American Academy of Arts and Letters Gold Medal for History.

BETHANNE KELLY PATRICK is the author of several books for young
readers, including *Abraham Lincoln* in the series CHILDHOODS OF THE
PRESIDENTS. She holds a master's degree in English from the
University of Virginia and specializes in middle-school curricula. She
is a freelance writer who lives with her husband and two daughters
in Virginia.